E REUBEN

The Runeforge Chronicles

Copyright © 2025 by E REUBEN

All rights reserved. No part of this publication may be reproduced, stored or transmitted in any form or by any means, electronic, mechanical, photocopying, recording, scanning, or otherwise without written permission from the publisher. It is illegal to copy this book, post it to a website, or distribute it by any other means without permission.

This novel is entirely a work of fiction. The names, characters and incidents portrayed in it are the work of the author's imagination. Any resemblance to actual persons, living or dead, events or localities is entirely coincidental.

E REUBEN asserts the moral right to be identified as the author of this work.

E REUBEN has no responsibility for the persistence or accuracy of URLs for external or third-party Internet Websites referred to in this publication and does not guarantee that any content on such Websites is, or will remain, accurate or appropriate.

Designations used by companies to distinguish their products are often claimed as trademarks. All brand names and product names used in this book and on its cover are trade names, service marks, trademarks and registered trademarks of their respective owners. The publishers and the book are not associated with any product or vendor mentioned in this book. None of the companies referenced within the book have endorsed the book.

First edition

This book was professionally typeset on Reedsy.
Find out more at reedsy.com

Contents

1	The Awakening of the Forge	1
2	The Map of Forgotten Realms	4
3	The Guardians of the Shattered Vale	7
4	The Trial of Echoes	11
5	The Heart of the Forgotten Keep	15
6	Into the Shifting Realms	19
7	The Forge of Fates	23
8	The Catalyst of Change	27
9	Echoes of the Fallen	31
10	The Dawn of the Rebirth	35

1

The Awakening of the Forge

The wind howled through the dense trees, carrying with it an unsettling chill that made the forest seem alive with whispered secrets. The towering pines bent under the pressure, their dark boughs shifting with every gust, creating shadows that seemed to writhe and move. In the midst of this eerie stillness, the sound of hooves crunching against the frosty underbrush was the only thing that could be heard for miles.

Liora, the young thief, crouched low in the saddle of her horse, her eyes scanning the horizon. The distant peaks of the mountains that had once been home to legends loomed before her, a dark reminder of the path she was about to embark on. The coldness in the air wasn't just the winter's touch—it was something far older, something forgotten.

"We're getting close," she murmured to herself, her voice barely rising above the sound of the wind.

Beside her, the disgraced mage, Eryndor, muttered something beneath his breath, eyes narrowed with suspicion. His hand, encased in a glove of intricate silver runes, rested lightly on the hilt of his staff, its crystal core pulsing faintly as though it too sensed the change in the air.

"There's a presence here," he said, more to himself than to Liora, but she caught the apprehension in his tone.

The two of them had been traveling together for weeks now, a strange alliance formed by necessity rather than trust. Liora was seeking the forgotten wealth of the ancient world, and Eryndor, though once a scholar of the arcane, had found himself exiled after a failed experiment that left his reputation in tatters. Now, both of them found themselves drawn to the same goal—an ancient relic hidden within the ruins of an abandoned city, deep in the heart of the wilderness. But it wasn't just any relic. It was the key to something far more powerful: the legendary Runeforge.

The Runeforge was an ancient, mythical forge said to be capable of creating weapons of unimaginable power, each imbued with the essence of the elements themselves. It was a place of untold mysteries, guarded for centuries by the most formidable of magical wards and hidden from those who sought its power. But Eryndor had discovered something—a fragment of a forgotten text—that hinted at its location.

"Do you feel that?" Liora asked, reining in her horse and glancing around nervously. Her hand reached instinctively for the dagger at her side, though she wasn't sure what threat she anticipated. The forest felt oppressive, as if it were holding its breath.

Eryndor nodded grimly. "The wards are stirring. We're not alone."

It was then that the trees ahead of them began to part, revealing an ancient structure half-buried in the earth and shrouded in ivy. The once-proud columns that had once held this place aloft now lay crumbled, and the walls were cracked and weathered by the passage of time. But there was something still hauntingly beautiful about it—the intricate runes carved into the stones, the symbols of old magic that pulsed faintly in the gloom.

Liora's breath caught in her throat as she dismounted from her horse, her feet touching the frozen ground with a quiet thud. The air here felt different, heavier, as though the very stones were alive with magic. She could almost hear the hum of power, distant but unmistakable.

"This is it," she whispered, her voice tinged with awe and fear. The ruins of the Runeforge had been the stuff of legends, something her grandmother had told her stories about, stories of warriors wielding weapons that could bend the very forces of nature to their will. To be standing here, at the very threshold of that myth, was almost too much to comprehend.

Eryndor stepped forward, his eyes gleaming with a mix of wonder and trepidation. "It's more than just a forge," he murmured, more to himself than to her. "It's a place of creation and destruction. A place where the very fabric of magic was woven into existence."

He reached out and placed his hand on one of the stone pillars, feeling the vibrations of the ancient magic coursing through it. For a moment, nothing happened. But then, as if the ruins themselves had been waiting for something, a low rumble echoed from deep within the ground.

The earth trembled beneath their feet, and the sky above darkened as clouds gathered overhead. A crackling energy filled the air, and Liora took an instinctive step back. "What's happening?" she asked, her voice tight with fear.

Eryndor's face was pale as he pulled his hand away from the stone. "The wards are awakening. It's been centuries since anyone dared come here."

Suddenly, a figure appeared in the shadows, stepping out from the darkened doorway of the forge. Tall, cloaked in midnight blue, with eyes that shimmered like molten gold, the figure seemed as much a part of the ruin as the stones themselves. The figure raised a hand, and the rumbling ceased.

"You seek the Runeforge," the figure's voice was like a whisper, but it resonated in their bones, as though it were not just spoken but *felt*. "But be warned, travelers. The forge is not kind to those who do not understand the price of its power."

Liora's heart pounded in her chest as she looked up at the stranger, who stood unmoving, their silhouette sharp against the darkening sky. She had known the risks of seeking the Runeforge, but hearing it spoken aloud made the gravity of their quest sink deep into her soul. There was no turning back now.

"We understand," Eryndor said, his voice steady but edged with uncertainty.

The figure's golden eyes flickered. "Then let the trial begin."

2

The Map of Forgotten Realms

The figure before them, cloaked in shadow and mystery, stood still as the world seemed to hold its breath. The ground beneath their feet thrummed with a silent power, the hum of ancient magic that reverberated through every stone of the forgotten ruins. Liora's hand instinctively tightened around the hilt of her dagger, though she knew, in that moment, that there was no weapon in the world that could truly prepare them for what lay ahead.

Eryndor, standing beside her, seemed more composed, his eyes flickering with a mixture of curiosity and wariness. The voice they had just heard echoed in his mind, and he tried to piece together the meaning of the stranger's words.

"The trial?" Liora's voice broke through the tense silence, cutting through the thick air between them. Her gaze was locked on the figure who stood like a specter in the doorway of the Runeforge.

The figure nodded once, a slow and deliberate motion, their golden eyes glimmering in the dim light. "The Runeforge does not give its power freely," the figure said. "To awaken its heart, to wield the weapons it forges, you must first prove yourselves worthy. You must find the pieces of the Runeforge Stone, scattered across the lands, each guarded by trials designed to test the very core of your being."

Liora exchanged a glance with Eryndor, her brow furrowed in thought. "And where do we start?" she asked, her voice steady despite the whirlwind of questions that flooded her mind.

The figure raised their hand again, and a soft glow emanated from the depths of their cloak. From within, a weathered scroll unfurled in the air between them, the parchment glowing faintly with an ethereal light. The scroll hovered for a moment, and then, with a swift motion, it dropped into Eryndor's hands.

"This map will guide you," the figure intoned. "But beware—those who seek the Runeforge are rarely the only ones who seek it."

Liora took a step closer, her eyes narrowing in suspicion. "What do you mean by that?" she asked, but the figure was already fading into the shadows, their voice carrying with it an almost imperceptible warning.

"The map will show you the way, but beware of the forces that will come after you. They will stop at nothing to claim the power of the Runeforge for themselves."

Before either of them could respond, the figure was gone, leaving only the faintest trace of their presence behind, like smoke dissipating into the air.

Eryndor unfurled the map carefully, his fingers tracing the edges of the ancient parchment. It was worn with age, its once-bright ink now faded and cracked, but the intricate symbols and lines remained sharp, as though time itself had little effect on the magic that infused the map.

Liora peered over his shoulder, her curiosity piqued. The map seemed to shift before her eyes, as though it were alive, the lands it depicted shifting and changing with every glance. She could see distant mountains, vast forests, and ancient ruins—each marked with cryptic symbols that she could not decipher. But at the center of it all, in bold, almost glowing runes, was the symbol of the Runeforge itself, a circle surrounded by intricate, swirling patterns. It was as if the map was pulling them toward a singular point.

"We need to find these places," Eryndor said quietly, his voice filled with a mixture of determination and uncertainty. "These trials… they're the key."

Liora nodded, her eyes scanning the map again. "And where do we start?" she asked, already anticipating the answer. The journey would be long, and the map provided only the vaguest of directions.

"There's a place marked here," Eryndor said, pointing to a remote island off the coast, far to the west. The island was marked by a strange symbol, unlike any other on the map. "It's called the Isle of Mirrors. The trial there is said to test the very soul of those who seek the Runeforge."

Liora frowned. "A trial of the soul?" The thought of a test so personal made her uneasy. She had little interest in facing her own inner demons, let alone in some distant, forgotten place. But she understood that there was no other choice. The Runeforge was too powerful, and if they were to stand any chance of wielding it, they had to prove themselves worthy.

"We'll need a ship," she said after a moment of silence. "And provisions. This journey won't be easy."

Eryndor nodded, folding the map carefully. "We'll make preparations," he agreed. "But we must be swift. The longer we wait, the more danger we're in. There are others out there who will stop at nothing to claim the power of the Runeforge."

Liora's thoughts drifted to the stranger's words. *Beware of the forces that will come after you.* She had no doubt that the Runeforge was more than just a simple forge—it was a weapon, a tool of unimaginable power, and there were bound to be those who would stop at nothing to claim it. But they couldn't let fear rule them. Not now.

She turned to Eryndor, her expression resolute. "Let's go. The Isle of Mirrors awaits."

The two of them gathered their things quickly, knowing that time was of the essence. As they made their way out of the ruins, the wind picked up once more, carrying with it a promise of what was to come. The journey ahead would be fraught with danger, but they both knew that there was no turning back now. The Runeforge was within their grasp, and the trials it demanded would shape their fates forever.

As they departed, the ancient ruins behind them seemed to whisper, as though the very stones knew that the quest for the Runeforge had just begun.

3

The Guardians of the Shattered Vale

The journey from the forgotten ruins of the Runeforge to the Isle of Mirrors was long and arduous, but it was nothing compared to the trials they had yet to face. After securing passage aboard a ship bound for the western coasts, Liora and Eryndor sailed for weeks through treacherous waters, their path often obscured by thick fogs and violent storms. But as they approached their destination, the weather cleared, revealing a land that seemed untouched by time—an ancient, wild place where nature itself had claimed dominion.

The Isle of Mirrors was just the first of many places the map would lead them, but they had not anticipated the dangers lurking closer to shore. As the ship dropped anchor in a small bay, Liora felt the weight of the island's silence pressing down on her. There were no signs of life, no distant calls of animals or the chatter of village folk—just the low hum of the earth and the soft ripple of waves against the shore. It was as though the land had not been disturbed in centuries.

"We're here," Eryndor said quietly, scanning the shores with cautious eyes. "This is the place. The Isle of Mirrors."

Liora's gaze lingered on the dense forest that stretched into the heart of the island, its towering trees like sentinels watching them from afar. "It's unnervingly quiet," she remarked. Her fingers itched for the comfort of her blade, though she didn't know what exactly to expect. The map had indicated this was where their first trial would unfold, but no description had been given—only that the trial was to test their very souls.

Without further word, they made their way onto the island, taking their first steps into the dark, thick forest. The ground beneath their feet was soft and damp, and the air was thick with an unnatural stillness. The trees loomed overhead, their twisted branches heavy with moss and leaves, blocking out most of the sunlight and casting long, ominous shadows.

It wasn't long before they came upon the first sign of the trial: the Shattered Vale. At the heart of the vale lay a series of jagged rocks and crumbled stone structures, the remnants of what appeared to be an ancient temple or fortress. What had once been a grand place now lay in ruins, as if some great force had torn it asunder. The broken stone and scattered rubble gave off a sense of desolation, as if this place had been abandoned for millennia.

"This is it," Eryndor muttered. "The Guardians are here. They protect the way forward."

Liora raised an eyebrow. "Guardians? I thought we were here to face a trial, not a battle."

Eryndor's eyes were grim. "The trial takes many forms. The Guardians of the Shattered Vale are not merely protectors of the path—they are the keepers of the trial. To move forward, we must face them. And they will test us in ways we cannot predict."

Before Liora could respond, a low, guttural sound echoed through the vale. It was a growl, deep and resonant, like the growl of a beast that had been awakened from a long slumber. From the shadows of the ruined temple, dark figures began to emerge. They were humanoid in shape, but their features were twisted—feral, inhuman. Their eyes glowed with an eerie, green light, and their skin was covered in rough, stone-like armor. These were no ordinary guardians.

"They are constructs of the earth itself," Eryndor said, his voice filled with awe. "Forged by ancient magic to defend this place."

The Guardians moved with unnatural speed, their movements quick and purposeful as they advanced toward Liora and Eryndor. They raised their weapons—massive stone axes and spears—each one etched with runes of power. The air shimmered with magic, and the ground beneath their feet trembled as the Guardians took their first steps into the vale.

Liora unsheathed her dagger, ready for whatever came. She wasn't sure what kind of trial this was, but she had faced more than her fair share of danger. Still, she couldn't shake the feeling that this was no ordinary battle. The Guardians didn't just fight to defeat—they fought to test.

As the first Guardian lunged at her, Liora spun, dodging the heavy swing of its stone axe. She ducked under its next strike, her movements fluid, like water flowing around a rock. With a swift twist of her wrist, she drove her dagger into the joint of the Guardian's armor, aiming for the gap between its chest and shoulder. The blade sank deep, but the Guardian barely flinched.

"These things are tough," Liora muttered under her breath, drawing back for another strike.

Eryndor, meanwhile, stood at a distance, his staff raised high as he muttered incantations under his breath. A surge of energy crackled from the staff, and with a flick of his wrist, a bolt of lightning shot from the tip, striking one of the Guardians directly in the chest. The stone creature staggered, but still it pressed forward, relentless.

"They're not going down easily," Eryndor said, frustration evident in his voice. "We need to find their weakness."

Liora's eyes darted to the ancient runes that adorned the Guardians' bodies. "The runes," she said suddenly. "They must be the key. If we can disable them..."

Eryndor's eyes widened as he realized what she meant. "Of course. The runes—they control the Guardians' magic. If we can break the seals, we can stop them."

But even as they formulated a plan, the Guardians seemed to sense their intent. One of the creatures lunged at Liora, knocking her to the ground. Its massive stone hand closed around her throat, squeezing the air from her lungs. She struggled beneath its weight, but it was too strong.

Eryndor's voice rang out in a desperate chant as he raised his staff higher, his eyes glowing with arcane power. The ground beneath the Guardians cracked and split, and suddenly, tendrils of magic shot from the earth, ensnaring the stone creatures in a web of crackling energy. The Guardians struggled, their movements slowed as the magic disrupted the runes etched into their bodies.

Liora took the opportunity to slip free, rolling away from the Guardian's grasp and reaching for her dagger. With a swift motion, she plunged the blade into the rune at the base of the creature's neck. There was a sudden, explosive crack as the stone armor shattered, and the Guardian collapsed into a pile of rubble.

Panting heavily, Liora stood, her eyes scanning the fallen guardians around her. Eryndor lowered his staff, the magic fading from the air. The trial, it seemed, was far from over—but they had passed the first test. The Guardians, now disarmed and broken, lay still.

"We've done it," Eryndor said, his voice filled with relief. But there was no time to rest. The vale still held its secrets, and the path forward was unclear. The trial of the Shattered Vale had only just begun.

Liora wiped the sweat from her brow, her expression hardening. "Let's move on," she said. "We've got a long way to go."

4

The Trial of Echoes

The Shattered Vale had been but a beginning—a mere whisper of the challenges that awaited them. As Liora and Eryndor pressed deeper into the island, their path now led them to a strange and unsettling place: a cavern, hidden beneath the ancient ruins, known only as the Trial of Echoes. The air grew heavier, denser, with each step they took, and the silence around them felt suffocating. It was as though the very walls of the cavern held their breath, waiting for something—someone—to disturb the stillness.

The entrance to the cavern was narrow, the stone walls slick with moisture and the faint smell of decay. Liora's hand instinctively went to her dagger as they descended into the darkness, the only light coming from the glowing runes on Eryndor's staff, casting eerie shadows on the walls. The deeper they went, the more it seemed as if the air itself vibrated with a strange resonance, an energy that thrummed beneath their feet.

"This place feels… wrong," Liora murmured, her voice barely a whisper as she moved forward. Her instincts, honed by years of surviving dangerous situations, were on high alert. There was something about the cavern, something that felt unnatural, as though it were a place suspended in time—a space where the past and the present intertwined.

Eryndor nodded, his eyes narrowing as he scanned their surroundings. "The Trial of Echoes is said to be a test of memory. But not just any memory. This is the kind of trial that forces you to confront your past, your deepest regrets, your greatest fears. It will make us relive moments we'd rather forget."

Liora's grip on her dagger tightened. She was no stranger to painful memories. She had lived through a past filled with loss, betrayal, and hard choices, but she had buried those memories deep within her, hoping they would never surface again. The idea of facing them head-on filled her with a cold dread, but there was no turning back now. She had come this far, and the Runeforge was within reach.

The cavern opened into a vast, domed chamber, the walls covered in intricate carvings that seemed to move and shift as they approached. The runes on the walls flickered like firelight, casting dancing shadows across the cavern. At the center of the chamber stood a pool of water, perfectly still, its surface reflecting the faint glow of the runes. But there was something else—something that wasn't quite right about the reflection.

Liora stepped closer to the pool, her reflection distorted, flickering like a broken image. As she reached the edge, the water began to ripple, and a voice echoed through the chamber, soft at first, like a whisper carried on the wind.

"Do you remember?"

Liora froze. The voice was familiar, yet not. It carried the weight of a thousand voices, each one a reflection of a forgotten moment. She looked to Eryndor, who stood beside her, his face pale, his eyes wide with an emotion she couldn't quite place.

"What is this?" Liora asked, her voice strained. "What's happening?"

Eryndor swallowed, his gaze fixed on the water. "This is the trial. The Echoes aren't just voices. They're manifestations of our past—our regrets, our mistakes. If we fail to confront them, we will be lost to the echoes forever."

Liora's heart pounded in her chest. The words seemed to ring in her ears, echoing against the walls of the cavern. The water rippled again, and the image in the pool shifted. She saw herself, younger, standing before a burning village. The flames reflected in her eyes, and the smell of smoke choked the air. Her hand trembled as she reached for a blade, the same blade that had been used in the battle, the same blade that had taken a life she would never forget.

"You killed him." The voice from the pool was sharp, accusing.

Liora stumbled back, her breath catching in her throat. The image in the water shifted again, showing the face of a young man—his eyes wide with shock, his blood staining the earth beneath him. She knew him, had known him once before, before the war had torn their lives apart. He had been a friend, a comrade in arms, and yet, in the heat of battle, she had struck him down, mistaking him for an enemy. His death had haunted her every night since.

"No," she whispered, shaking her head, trying to break free from the vision. "It wasn't my fault. I didn't mean to…"

But the voice only grew louder. *"You killed him. You were the one who betrayed him. You are the cause of his death."*

Liora's knees buckled beneath her as the weight of the memory bore down on her. She had lived with the guilt for years, but she had buried it, pretending it didn't matter, convincing herself that she had done what was necessary. But now, in the face of the Echoes, it was all too real, too vivid. She could see his face, could feel the blood on her hands once again.

Eryndor's voice cut through the haze of her memories. "Liora, listen to me! This is the trial. You have to face it. You can't let the Echoes control you."

Liora looked up at him, her vision blurred by tears she hadn't realized were falling. She wanted to deny it, to turn away from the guilt that consumed her, but the voice in the pool wouldn't let her. It was as if the Echoes were reaching into her soul, pulling out every dark secret, every unspoken fear.

"You have to confront the truth," Eryndor urged. "Look at it. You didn't kill him on purpose. You were caught in the chaos of battle. This is the past, Liora. It's not who you are now."

The words seemed to sink into her mind, and for a moment, the world around her fell silent. She stared into the water, seeing her reflection once again. This time, it was different—clearer. She saw the pain in her eyes, the guilt that had weighed her down, but she also saw the strength that had emerged from the ashes of her past. She had made mistakes, but she had grown from them. She had chosen a different path, one that led her here, to this moment.

With a deep breath, Liora stepped forward, her hand outstretched toward the water. The voice in the pool faltered, its power waning as she embraced the truth. The surface of the water calmed, and the reflection of the young man faded into nothingness.

The chamber fell silent, the oppressive weight of the trial lifting. The Echoes had been silenced.

Eryndor stepped up beside her, his eyes filled with understanding. "You did it," he said quietly. "You faced it."

Liora nodded, wiping the tears from her face. The trial had been harder than anything she had ever faced, but she knew now that she was not defined by the past. The Runeforge still awaited them, but the journey had become more than just a quest for power. It had become a path to redemption. And with each step they took, they were growing stronger—together.

5

The Heart of the Forgotten Keep

The air was thick with the scent of damp earth and aged stone as Liora and Eryndor trekked further into the heart of the island. The Trial of Echoes had left them both exhausted, but their path was far from over. The map they had been given—the one leading to the legendary Runeforge—was beginning to show them fragments of a deeper truth, a truth that tied together forgotten histories and long-buried secrets. Now, the next phase of their journey awaited them in the ruins of the Forgotten Keep.

The Keep stood at the summit of a jagged mountain, its ancient spires cutting into the sky like broken fingers. It was said to be the final resting place of the last of the Runemasters, those who had crafted the magic that bound the land together. But over the centuries, the Keep had fallen into ruin, its halls now home to dark creatures and lingering malevolence. It was a place where time had eroded both stone and memory, and where even the bravest adventurers had been lost forever.

Liora and Eryndor made their way through the dense forest that led to the base of the mountain, the trees growing increasingly twisted the closer they came to their destination. Strange, low-hanging vines, their leaves blackened and withered, draped from the branches like the remnants of some forgotten ritual. The birds that had once called this forest home were eerily absent, replaced by the sounds of whispers that seemed to emanate from the very earth beneath their feet.

"This is it," Eryndor said, his voice low as he surveyed the landscape ahead. "The Forgotten Keep. We are close now."

Liora nodded, her hand resting on the hilt of her dagger. The ominous feeling she had felt ever since they entered the island had only grown stronger. Something was watching them, something ancient and malevolent, lurking just beyond the veil of reality. But there was no turning back now. The map's markings had led them here, and she knew they could not afford to falter.

The path up the mountain was treacherous, winding its way through steep cliffs and dense undergrowth. They scaled narrow ledges, crossing bridges of crumbling stone, their every step echoing through the vast emptiness. As they reached the summit, the sky seemed to darken, as though the very heavens themselves were retreating from the presence of the Keep. The ruins loomed before them, its gates half-buried in the rock, as if the earth itself had tried to swallow it whole.

"This is where it ends," Liora said, her voice filled with both awe and apprehension.

Eryndor's gaze was fixed on the Keep. "No. This is where it begins."

They pushed forward, entering the shattered remains of the fortress. The interior was even more desolate than the exterior, the walls lined with the skeletal remains of what had once been the Keep's inhabitants—warriors, scholars, and sages who had once served the Runemasters. Their bones were now part of the very stone that surrounded them, twisted and contorted as if they had been caught in some terrible, inescapable trap.

Liora's eyes scanned the surroundings, taking in the faded murals and broken statues that had once adorned the walls. Each was a testament to a forgotten time—an era of magic and power that had long since been extinguished. Yet, there was a feeling that lingered here, an energy that pulsed just beneath the surface of the ruins.

At the center of the Keep stood an enormous stone archway, its edges etched with symbols Liora could not understand. It was as if the archway itself was a gateway to another world—an entrance to a place where the boundaries between time and space no longer held sway. The air around it shimmered, and a low hum seemed to reverberate from the very stones beneath their feet.

"This is it," Eryndor whispered, his voice filled with awe and reverence. "The Heart of the Forgotten Keep."

Liora stepped forward, her hand brushing against the cold surface of the archway. The hum grew louder, vibrating through her body, and for a moment, she felt as though she were being pulled into the very fabric of the Keep itself. But she quickly shook off the sensation, her resolve hardening. The map had led them here for a reason, and this was the place where they would discover the final piece of the puzzle.

Suddenly, the archway flared to life, its runes glowing with an intense, otherworldly light. The air around them crackled with energy as a figure stepped through the portal—tall, cloaked in tattered robes, with eyes that glowed like embers. His presence was both commanding and terrifying, and for a moment, Liora felt the overwhelming urge to turn and flee.

The figure spoke in a voice that was both ancient and powerful. "You have come far, but your journey is not yet complete. The Runeforge lies beyond this place, but to enter, you must first pass the final trial."

Liora's heart raced as she took a step forward, her hand resting on the hilt of her dagger. "What do you want from us?" she demanded.

The figure's eyes locked onto hers, and for a moment, it felt as if he could see straight into her soul. "I am the Keeper of the Keep," he said, his voice a soft whisper that echoed through the vast chamber. "I have watched over this place for centuries, waiting for those worthy of entering the Runeforge. But few have been able to overcome the final trial. And even fewer have survived."

Eryndor stepped forward, his staff raised in a gesture of both defiance and respect. "What is the trial?" he asked, his voice steady but filled with uncertainty.

The Keeper's lips curled into a faint smile. "The trial is one of the mind and spirit, for the Runeforge will not grant its power to those who cannot control themselves. You will face your deepest fears, your darkest desires, and your greatest regrets. Only by confronting them can you prove yourselves worthy."

Liora's pulse quickened. She had faced trials before, but none like this. The Keeper's words echoed in her mind, and she knew that the challenge ahead would be unlike anything they had ever experienced.

The Keeper extended a hand toward the archway. "Step forward, if you dare. The Runeforge awaits, but only those who are truly ready may claim its power."

Without another word, the Keeper dissolved into the shadows, leaving only the flickering light of the archway behind him. Liora exchanged a glance with Eryndor, her mind racing. The path ahead was shrouded in uncertainty, but one thing was clear: whatever awaited them beyond the arch would be the ultimate test. The Heart of the Forgotten Keep had spoken, and now, they had no choice but to follow.

Taking a deep breath, Liora stepped forward, her heart pounding in her chest. The air around the archway grew thick, the world around them warping and twisting. Whatever lay ahead, she was ready. She had come this far. And she would not turn back now.

6

Into the Shifting Realms

The world around Liora and Eryndor shifted violently as they stepped through the portal, the air pulsing with a strange energy. One moment, they were standing in the desolate ruins of the Forgotten Keep, the next, they were plunged into an expanse of swirling mists and fractured landscapes. The earth beneath their feet felt unstable, as though the very ground was not sure whether it wished to exist or not. It was as if the laws of nature had been undone, and now only chaos ruled.

Liora blinked, trying to adjust to the sudden change. The mist swirled around her, thick and gray, distorting her vision. Shadows seemed to dance within the fog, flickering like ghosts, and the silence was deafening—oppressive, as if even sound had lost its way here. Eryndor stood by her side, his staff glowing softly, the only constant in the disorienting swirl of nothingness.

"What… is this place?" Liora asked, her voice trembling with uncertainty. She had expected trials, had expected challenges, but this… this felt different. It wasn't like anything she had ever encountered before.

Eryndor's brow furrowed as he surveyed the shifting surroundings. "This is the Shifting Realms," he said quietly, his tone heavy with knowledge and caution. "A place between worlds, where the boundaries of reality are thin. It is said to be a mirror of the soul, where the deepest fears and desires of those who enter it take form. But it is also a place where nothing is certain. The landscape constantly changes, and the rules that govern it are unpredictable."

Liora felt a chill run down her spine. She had faced physical battles, fought enemies in the heat of war, but this was something entirely different. The Shifting Realms were not a place of monsters or armies; they were a place of the mind. And if Eryndor was right, whatever awaited them here would not be fought with blades or magic, but with their very selves.

"Do we just… walk through it?" she asked, though the question felt almost absurd in the face of such an intangible enemy. How could they even begin to navigate a realm that had no rules, no solid ground to stand on?

"We must endure the trial," Eryndor replied. "We are being tested. To reach the heart of the Runeforge, we must confront what lies hidden within us—our deepest truths. But remember, we cannot simply fight what appears. We must face it, accept it, and in doing so, we will find our way."

Liora's thoughts raced as she looked around. In the shifting mist, strange shapes began to take form. The shadows coalesced into faint figures—humanoids, twisted and contorted, their faces obscured, their eyes hollow. They loomed over them, silent, as if waiting for the right moment to strike. Yet, Liora felt no immediate threat from them. Instead, it was the presence of their gaze, the weight of being observed, that unnerved her.

"They're not real," Liora muttered, more to herself than to Eryndor. "Are they?"

"No," Eryndor replied, his voice steady despite the growing tension. "But they are reflections. You will see things here—visions, memories, fears—that you must face. Do not let them control you."

Liora's heart pounded as she glanced again at the figures. One stepped closer, its form growing more distinct. The mist seemed to part as if the figure was slicing through it, revealing a tall man dressed in armor, his face hidden by a dark hood. His presence sent a jolt through Liora's chest, for the figure was eerily familiar.

It was her father.

"Father?" she whispered, her voice trembling with disbelief. The man in the mist was impossibly tall, his face obscured by shadows, but she knew that voice. The voice that had once held authority, that had shaped her into the person she had become. Her father had been a warrior, a leader, a man of strength. But his death had been shrouded in mystery, and the grief of losing him had been the catalyst for her journey. She had buried the pain, refusing to let it define her—but here, in the Shifting Realms, the pain resurfaced, raw and unfiltered.

"Liora," the figure's voice boomed, low and commanding. "You failed me."

Her breath caught in her throat. "No. No, I didn't."

The mist began to swirl faster, pressing in on her. "You couldn't protect me. You couldn't protect our people. You abandoned us when we needed you most."

Tears welled up in Liora's eyes. She had never truly faced the guilt she felt over her father's death. It had been a tragic, senseless loss, but she had never allowed herself to process the anger and grief. She had pushed forward, determined not to let emotion slow her down. But now, in this place, it was all coming to the surface.

"You were weak," the figure's voice continued, now filled with disdain. "You were never strong enough to carry on our legacy."

Liora took a step back, shaking her head. "No… I didn't abandon you."

The figure raised a hand, as if to strike her, but she stood firm, her chest rising and falling rapidly. She had to face this—had to stop running from it. Her father's expectations had always been too high, his burdens too great. But she had never let go of the guilt of his death. Here, in the Shifting Realms, she was forced to confront the truth: she had done the best she could. She had loved him. But in the end, she had lost him, and that was a pain she couldn't undo.

"I couldn't save you," she whispered, her voice breaking. "But I am strong enough now."

The figure paused, and for a moment, Liora thought the world would collapse around her. The mist swirled more violently, but then, as if it had never been there, the figure of her father began to dissipate, melting away into the mist. The tension in the air lifted, and the figures that had once surrounded them disappeared as well.

Eryndor stood beside her, his gaze solemn but supportive. "You faced it," he said quietly. "You faced the truth."

Liora nodded, her breath still unsteady. The trial wasn't over, and she knew more challenges awaited. But for the first time, she felt a weight lifting from her chest. She had faced her fear, her guilt, and it no longer held the same power over her. The Shifting Realms had tested her, but she had endured. The mist around them had calmed, and in the distance, she could see a flicker of light—something stable, something real.

"The Runeforge is near," Eryndor said. "We must move forward. Together."

With a final glance at the dissipating mist, Liora nodded. The trial was far from over, but she had passed this test. And with Eryndor by her side, there was nothing they couldn't face.

The Shifting Realms would not claim them. Not today.

7

The Forge of Fates

The fog lifted, revealing the next phase of their journey: a vast, desolate landscape stretching beyond the horizon. Liora and Eryndor stood at the edge of a towering cliff, the ground beneath their feet cracked and broken, as if some great force had once torn it apart. A thick, sulfurous wind howled across the barren plains, whipping up loose stones and sending them skittering through the air. The air tasted metallic, and the skies above were an unnatural shade of blood red, casting an eerie glow across the land. In the distance, they could see the faint outline of something enormous, a structure that loomed in the center of the wasteland like an ancient beast waiting to awaken.

"The Runeforge," Liora whispered, her voice tinged with awe. The structure in the distance was unmistakable—massive, ancient, and somehow alive. The heat from it seemed to radiate even from this distance, and though they had not yet set foot within its bounds, Liora could feel its power calling to her, a force that resonated deep within her bones.

Eryndor, ever the cautious guide, studied the surroundings carefully. "This is the Forge of Fates," he said, his tone grave. "It is not a place for the fainthearted. Legends speak of the power it holds, but also of the dangers it harbors. It will test more than your strength. It will test your very soul."

Liora's hand instinctively tightened around the hilt of her dagger. They had faced countless trials, but this—this was something different. The Runeforge wasn't just a physical challenge. It was a crucible where destinies were forged and unmade, where lives were rewritten with a single stroke. She had come too far to falter now.

"Let's move," she said, her voice firm. She wasn't about to back down, not when she had come this far. And certainly not when the answers she sought—answers about her past, her father, and the Runeforge—were so close.

The journey toward the Runeforge felt endless, the distance between them and the structure deceptive. With every step, the terrain grew harsher, the winds more violent. A strange static filled the air, as though they were walking through a barrier that pushed against them, forcing them to exert every ounce of their strength just to keep moving forward. The very ground beneath their feet seemed to shift, as if the landscape itself was alive, watching them with a malice of its own.

When they finally reached the entrance of the Runeforge, it was even more awe-inspiring than they could have imagined. Towering obsidian pillars lined the path, inscribed with runes that seemed to pulse with an ancient, unspoken power. The gates of the Forge were massive, forged from blackened steel, and etched with symbols that spoke of forgotten gods and long-lost legends. The gates groaned and rumbled as they slowly began to open, as if they had not been disturbed in centuries.

"You're here," a voice boomed, deep and resonant, emanating from the heart of the Forge itself. The words reverberated through the air, shaking the very ground beneath their feet. "But do you truly understand what you seek?"

Liora and Eryndor exchanged wary glances. The voice—intangible, yet powerful—seemed to come from everywhere and nowhere at once. It was the voice of the Forge itself, or perhaps something that dwelled within its ancient walls.

"We seek the truth," Liora called out, her voice steady despite the overwhelming presence of the voice. "We seek the power of the Runeforge."

The ground beneath them trembled again, the gates fully opening with a sudden, deafening roar. Through the gates, they could see a vast chamber, its ceiling lost in shadow, its walls lined with hundreds of glowing forges. Each forge burned with a strange, otherworldly fire, casting the room in an unearthly glow. But what caught their attention was the massive forge at the center, larger than any other, its flames roaring with a heat that could be felt even from this distance.

At the heart of the central forge stood an enormous figure, tall and imposing, its form flickering in and out of existence like a mirage. It was an entity made of flame and shadow, a being that seemed to defy the very laws of nature. The figure's eyes burned with an unearthly light, and as it spoke, its voice was a low, commanding rumble, like the sound of molten metal being poured into a forge.

"Who dares enter the Forge of Fates?" the figure intoned, its gaze settling on Liora and Eryndor.

"We are Liora and Eryndor," Liora declared, her heart pounding. "We seek the Runeforge. We have come to claim its power."

The figure seemed to consider them for a moment, its eyes narrowing. "Power, you say? You seek the power of the Forge, but power comes with a price. The Runeforge does not grant its blessings to just any soul. It demands a sacrifice. A soul forged in fire. A destiny sealed in flame."

Liora's heart skipped a beat. She had known that there would be a price to pay for entering the Runeforge, but she hadn't expected this. What kind of sacrifice would the Forge demand? And more importantly, was she willing to pay that price?

The figure's voice cut through her thoughts. "Your path has led you here, but the choice is yours. To claim the power of the Runeforge, you must face your deepest fear, your most profound regret. Only then can you shape your fate. Only then can you wield the power that lies within this place."

Liora swallowed hard, her thoughts racing. She had already faced so much—her father's death, the trials in the Shifting Realms, her doubts, her fears. But now, in the heart of the Runeforge, she was being asked to confront something even more personal, more profound.

Eryndor stepped forward, his voice steady. "We are ready. We have come this far. We will face whatever it is that the Forge demands."

The figure in the center of the forge nodded slowly. "Very well," it said, its voice softening for the first time. "Then let the forging of your fate begin."

With a motion that was both fluid and abrupt, the figure extended its hand toward Liora. In an instant, the world around them shifted once again. The chamber of the Runeforge melted away, and Liora found herself standing alone in a vast, endless void. The air was cold, oppressive, and silent. The only thing that existed was her. And the shadow that loomed ahead.

A familiar voice echoed from the darkness, a voice that pierced through her very being. "You are nothing. You will always be nothing."

Liora's heart sank as the shadow took form, revealing the figure of her father. But this was not the father she had known. This was a twisted version of him, a cruel mockery of the man she had once admired.

"You failed me," the shadow of her father hissed. "You were weak. You could not save me, and now you are here, seeking to claim what is not yours."

Liora clenched her fists, her breath coming in short gasps. "No," she whispered. "I am not weak."

The shadow's laugh was hollow and cruel. "Then prove it. Face your fear. Show me you are strong enough to claim your destiny."

With that, the shadow lunged at her, its cold hands reaching for her throat. Fear surged through her, but Liora refused to back down. This was her trial. This was the final test. She would face her father's expectations, her own guilt, and emerge stronger.

As the shadow closed in, Liora stood her ground. "I will not be defined by my past. I will forge my own fate."

And with that declaration, the shadow dissipated into nothingness, leaving Liora standing alone once more. The cold void melted away, and the familiar warmth of the Runeforge surrounded her. She had passed the trial.

She was ready.

The figure in the center of the forge nodded once again. "You have faced your fear and conquered it. The power of the Runeforge is now yours to command."

8

The Catalyst of Change

Liora stood at the threshold of the Runeforge, her heart pounding with the weight of what had just transpired. The forge's flames danced wildly, casting eerie shadows across the darkened chamber. The power of the Runeforge surged through her veins, an energy unlike anything she had ever felt before—raw, unrelenting, and alive. The taste of it lingered in her mouth, metallic and charged with a thousand possibilities. The sacrifice had been made, the test passed, but the price—she could feel it in her bones—had left its mark.

Eryndor stepped up beside her, his expression unreadable as he studied her. His eyes flicked briefly to the figure still looming at the center of the forge, its fiery form pulsating with energy. The silence that had fallen between them was thick, but it was not uncomfortable. There was an understanding now, a knowing that they had reached a pivotal moment in their journey.

"You've done it," Eryndor said softly, his voice low but filled with awe.

Liora nodded, though her thoughts were scattered, still trying to process the trial she had just endured. Facing her father's shadow had been more than a mere test of courage. It had been a reckoning, forcing her to confront not just her past, but the burdens she had carried for so long. Her father's death, her failure to save him, the fear of never living up to the legacy he had left behind—all of it had come crashing down in that moment. But now, standing here in the heart of the Runeforge, she understood something. The past did not define her. She was not bound by her regrets or by what others had expected of her. She was her own person. She could shape her own destiny.

The figure in the center of the forge spoke, its voice like the crackle of flames, low and unearthly. "You have forged your destiny in the flames of the past. But now, the future awaits."

Liora turned toward it, her expression steady. "What do you mean?" she asked, her voice strong.

The figure's glowing eyes met hers, and for a moment, it seemed as though the very air around them thickened with the weight of its answer. "The power of the Runeforge is not just a weapon. It is a catalyst—a force of change that can alter the fabric of reality itself. It can create. It can destroy. It can reshape the world as you see fit."

Liora's breath caught in her throat. She had always known that the Runeforge held immense power, but this—this was beyond anything she had imagined. To reshape the world? It was almost too much to comprehend. Her gaze flickered to Eryndor, who was watching her closely, his brow furrowed with concern.

"How do I control it?" she asked, the question burning in her chest.

The figure's form rippled, the flames around it shifting as if to answer her. "Control is an illusion," it replied. "You do not control the power. You harness it. You focus it. And most importantly, you must choose how to wield it. The path you walk from here will shape the world, but be warned—every choice carries a consequence."

Liora felt a chill seep into her bones. Consequence. She had already paid a price, but this—this was the true weight of the power she now wielded. It wasn't just about defeating enemies or achieving her goals. The very act of shaping the future would ripple through time, affecting countless lives.

"What must I do now?" she asked, her voice steady despite the storm of thoughts raging in her mind.

The figure gestured to the forge, the flames dancing in response. "The forge has been ignited. The spark has been lit. But it is you who must now set the course. Seek the others who will walk beside you. Find the ones who will guide you in this new world. You are not alone in this journey. The choices ahead will require allies. Together, you will either bring salvation or doom."

Liora's heart raced at the mention of allies. She had already lost so much, and though Eryndor stood by her now, she knew that she could not face the challenges ahead without more than just him. The weight of responsibility pressed down on her chest. She wasn't just a survivor now. She was the catalyst for something far larger than herself.

"I understand," she said quietly, her voice filled with a new determination.

The figure's eyes glowed brighter, almost as though it were pleased with her response. "Good," it said. "Then go forth. The world awaits your choice."

With that, the flames in the center of the forge flared, and the figure seemed to dissolve into the fire itself, leaving only the heat and the crackling embers behind. The forge, once a place of dark and mysterious power, now felt strangely alive, pulsing with an energy that seemed to resonate with Liora's very being.

Eryndor stepped forward, his expression somber. "The world will not wait for us," he said, his tone grave. "We must move quickly. The forces that seek to control this power will not be slow to act."

Liora nodded, her mind already turning to the next steps of their journey. She knew that the path ahead would not be easy. There were enemies to face, secrets to uncover, and choices that would test every fiber of her being. But now, with the power of the Runeforge at her command, she had the strength to shape her destiny—and the world's—according to her will.

"I won't waste any more time," Liora said, her voice steady, filled with the fire of newfound purpose. "We have to find the others. The ones who can help us understand the true scope of what we're dealing with."

Eryndor's expression softened, a hint of admiration in his eyes. "Then we begin."

Together, they turned away from the heart of the Runeforge, leaving the flames behind them as they set forth on their new journey. The world outside was vast, filled with dangers and uncertainty, but with the power of the Runeforge coursing through her, Liora knew she was ready. She would face whatever came next—not as the daughter of a fallen hero, not as a mere survivor, but as the one who would decide the fate of all.

The Runeforge had awakened. And with it, so had she.

9

Echoes of the Fallen

The landscape outside the Runeforge was nothing like they had imagined. What should have been a thriving, vibrant world lay beneath a sky thick with ashen clouds, the air heavy with the weight of a thousand unshed tears. The land was scarred, as if some great war had left its mark—cracks ran through the earth like deep wounds, and the remnants of ruined cities lay buried beneath layers of dust and ash. The distant mountains, once towering and proud, were now mere shadows of their former selves, their peaks lost in the ominous clouds.

Liora stood at the edge of the desolation, the weight of the power she now carried pressing down on her shoulders. She had thought she understood what it meant to hold the power of the Runeforge, but now, in the face of this ruined world, she felt its true burden. The Forge had granted her the ability to shape destiny, to change the course of history, but it had also revealed something far more terrifying: the world was already broken, and no power, no matter how great, could heal it without cost.

Eryndor, who had been silent since they left the heart of the Forge, spoke now, his voice low and filled with concern. "This land… it is not what it should be. The Runeforge's power—it's not enough to mend the damage."

Liora's gaze swept over the horizon, her thoughts racing. She could feel the truth of his words deep within her, a gnawing sensation that told her this journey was far from over. The Runeforge had given her the ability to change things, yes, but it had not given her the knowledge of what to change, or how. The world was broken, and she had no idea where to begin.

"We'll figure it out," she said, though even to herself, her words felt hollow. The land before her seemed like a graveyard, and the very thought of attempting to repair it felt like an impossible task. But she couldn't afford to be weak now. Not when the world was on the edge of collapse. She had made her choice. She had to follow through.

Eryndor placed a hand on her shoulder, his touch grounding. "Liora, we're not alone in this. Remember that."

She nodded, though her mind was already elsewhere. Her thoughts were filled with the cryptic words of the figure at the Runeforge. The power to reshape the world, to forge a new destiny—it was within her reach. But the figure had said one thing that still haunted her: *"Every choice carries a consequence."*

"Do you hear that?" Eryndor's voice cut through her thoughts, sharp and alert.

Liora's hand instinctively went to the hilt of her dagger as she turned toward the sound. The wind had picked up, stirring the ash around them in swirling patterns. From the distance, faint echoes reached her ears—whispers carried on the wind, voices that seemed to cry out in agony.

"Voices," she said, narrowing her eyes. She could hear them now too, faint but unmistakable. "Do you think it's the spirits of the fallen?"

"It could be," Eryndor replied, his gaze scanning the horizon. "But we should be cautious. Not all spirits are harmless."

Liora swallowed, the weight of his words settling over her. They had already faced one trial in the Runeforge, but this—this felt different. The voices, distant yet filled with desperation, pulled at her, beckoning her forward. She had to know what they were, had to understand if they were a sign or a warning. She couldn't ignore it.

"Let's go," she said, her voice firm. "We need answers."

They moved cautiously through the barren land, the whispers growing louder with every step they took. The air grew colder, the temperature dropping rapidly as they approached the source of the voices. Liora felt an unfamiliar sensation crawl up her spine, a sense of dread creeping into her heart. The voices were no longer distant; they were here, surrounding them, echoing through the very air they breathed.

It wasn't until they reached the edge of a vast, empty plain that Liora saw them—the shadows.

At first, they were just flickers in the corner of her vision, brief flashes of movement, but then they solidified into shapes—figures cloaked in tattered robes, their faces hidden in the shadows. They moved slowly, like phantoms, their eyes glowing faintly with a spectral light. The whispers were louder now, their words unintelligible but undeniably filled with sorrow.

Liora stopped, her hand gripping the hilt of her dagger tightly. She could feel the power of the Runeforge within her, but this—this was something different. The spirits before her were not of the living, yet they exuded a sense of longing and pain that was palpable. Their presence was a physical weight, pressing down on her chest.

Eryndor stepped forward, his voice calm but cautious. "Who are you?"

The nearest spirit stopped, its head tilting in their direction. For a long moment, there was only silence, and then the voice of the spirit cut through the stillness, a low and hollow whisper. "We are the Echoes… the lost ones. The ones forgotten."

Liora's heart skipped a beat. "Forgotten? Forgotten by whom?"

The spirit's glowing eyes seemed to burn with an intensity that sent shivers down her spine. "Forgotten by time. By the world. We were once part of something greater, but now… now we are adrift. Bound to this place, caught between worlds."

A chill ran through Liora as the words sank in. These spirits, these Echoes, were not just the souls of the departed. They were remnants of something lost, caught in a state of limbo. And somehow, they were tied to the destruction she had witnessed.

"What do you want from us?" Liora asked, her voice steady, though her heart was pounding.

The spirit's head tilted again, its eyes narrowing as though it was considering her words. "We seek release," it whispered. "The land is broken, and so are we. But you... you carry the power of the Runeforge. You could undo what was done. You could restore us. Restore the world."

Liora's breath caught in her throat. The weight of the moment hung heavy around her. The spirits before her were not just seeking peace for themselves—they were calling her to act. They had been forgotten, abandoned by time itself, and now they were turning to her, the one who wielded the power to reshape the world.

"I... I don't know how," Liora whispered, her voice barely audible.

The spirit's eyes softened, and for a fleeting moment, Liora saw a glimpse of something beyond the darkness—a spark of hope. "You know more than you think. You hold the key, Liora. You hold the power to change this world, to restore what was lost."

The wind howled, and the spirits began to fade, their voices dissolving into the wind. The last words that lingered in the air were a plea, one that would follow Liora for the rest of her journey.

"Do not forget us, Liora. Do not let the world forget."

As the last of the spirits vanished, Liora stood in silence, the weight of their words heavy in her heart. She had come to the Runeforge seeking answers, seeking power. But what she had found was something far greater—the responsibility to heal a world on the brink of collapse, and to remember the forgotten. The road ahead was uncertain, and the price of her power was still unclear, but she knew one thing for certain: she could not walk away from this.

Not now. Not ever.

10

The Dawn of the Rebirth

The world had changed, though not in the way Liora had hoped. It was still scarred, still broken in many places, but something within the land had begun to stir—something that hadn't been felt in centuries. The Runeforge's power had ignited a spark, a fragile hope that things could be mended, that the world might one day rise from its ashes.

Liora stood on the edge of the now-infamous plateau, the sun's first rays casting a golden glow across the horizon. The ruins of the cities that had once dominated this land were still there, weathered and decayed, but they no longer felt as oppressive. They were no longer reminders of failure, but of a time lost to history—pieces of a puzzle that, when put together, would reveal something far more enduring.

Eryndor stood beside her, his usual stoic expression softened by the quiet of the morning. The remnants of their journey were evident in both their faces—dark circles under their eyes, the weight of battles fought, the scars of choices made—but also in their posture. They had become something more than mere survivors. They had become leaders, stewards of the world's fragile future.

"It's strange," Liora said, her voice barely above a whisper. "It feels like the land is… waking up."

Eryndor's gaze never left the horizon, but there was a slight nod. "It is. The power of the Runeforge courses through the earth itself now. It will take time, but the rebirth has already begun."

Liora looked down at her hands, the same hands that had once gripped the dagger with fear and uncertainty. Now, those hands felt different—stronger, more confident. They had shaped the future, for better or worse. The echoes of the spirits had not been silenced, nor had the consequences of her actions been washed away. But she had done something that many before her had failed to do: she had dared to make the choice to act.

Behind her, the remaining members of their group—those who had rallied to her side through thick and thin—had begun to gather. The journey had not been easy, and it had cost them more than they had ever anticipated. But they were still standing, still united by the same purpose: to rebuild the broken world.

Talin, the fiery warrior whose blade had cleaved through countless foes, was the first to speak. His voice was gruff, but there was a glimmer of something more in it now—hope. "You've done it, Liora. We've done it. The Forge was a means to an end, but it's what comes next that matters."

Liora turned to face him, her heart swelling with gratitude. "We all did it," she said quietly. "None of this would have been possible without all of you."

The others nodded, acknowledging the truth in her words. The small group that had once been strangers, brought together by fate and necessity, had become more than allies. They had become a family. And like any family, they had learned to carry one another's burdens, to pick each other up when the weight of the world felt too much to bear.

Zara, the skilled healer who had bound their wounds both physical and emotional, stepped forward with a soft smile. "The land will heal, Liora. But it will take time. We must be patient, even as we work tirelessly to restore what was lost. The scars are deep, but not permanent."

Liora nodded, the truth of Zara's words settling into her bones. Patience was a virtue she had not always embraced, but she knew now that it would be essential. The land was changing, yes, but it would require steady hands and kind hearts to guide it back to its former glory. It was a task that would span generations, not just one.

As the sun rose higher in the sky, the group gathered their belongings and began the journey back to the heart of the land, where the rebuilding would begin in earnest. They would have to be strategic, to rebuild from the ground up. But they were not starting from nothing. The Runeforge had granted them something invaluable: the knowledge that it was possible to rebuild, to reshape the world, and to do so with hope.

But even as they set off, Liora could feel the weight of what lay ahead. The consequences of her choices had yet to be fully realized, and there would be those who would resist the changes they sought to bring. Not everyone would welcome the idea of a new world—a world shaped by the power of the Runeforge. But Liora knew one thing for sure: they could not stand idly by. They had to fight for this future. It was the only one worth having.

The winds had shifted as well, carrying with them the scent of rain—a symbol of new beginnings. Liora closed her eyes for a moment, breathing in the air deeply, feeling the pulse of the land beneath her feet. The weight of the power she held was not a burden anymore. It was a gift, one that came with the understanding that true power was not in domination or destruction, but in creation and restoration.

Behind her, Eryndor's voice broke the silence. "The world is waking up, Liora. And so are we."

Liora turned to him, meeting his gaze with newfound determination. "We've only just begun."

And so, the first steps of their new journey began. The world, broken and forgotten, had begun to stir. But this time, Liora and her companions would be ready. They would guide it, rebuild it, and make sure it never fell to ruin again. For they had learned the most important lesson of all: the world was not just shaped by the power of the Runeforge, but by the choices of those who wielded it. And as long as they remained steadfast, the dawn of the rebirth would not be just a hope—it would be a reality.

Liora took a final glance at the horizon, where the first light of dawn had broken through the clouds, and a quiet sense of peace settled over her heart. The path ahead was uncertain, but she was no longer afraid. With her companions by her side, and the power of the Runeforge in her grasp, she was ready to face whatever came next. The world was waking up. And she would walk with it, into the future, as its guardian.